HOW TO
WITNESS
TO
ANYONE

Titles by R. A. Torrey

HOW TO
WITNESS
TO
ANYONE

COMPILED BY
R.A. TORREY

Whitaker House

Publisher's note:
This edition from Whitaker House has been updated for
the modern reader. Words, expressions, and sentence
structure have been revised for clarity and readability.

Unless otherwise indicated, all Scripture quotations
are taken from the King James Version (KJV) of
the Holy Bible.

HOW TO WITNESS TO ANYONE

ISBN-13: 978-0-88368-170-1
ISBN-10: 0-88368-170-6
Printed in the United States of America
© 1984 by Whitaker House

Whitaker House
1030 Hunt Valley Circle
New Kensington, PA 15068
www.whitakerhouse.com

13 14 15 16 17 18 19 20 ␣␣␣ 14 13 12 11 10 09 08 07

Contents

Introduction

In a compelling passage of Scripture in the book of Matthew, Jesus told His disciples:

The harvest truly is plenteous, but the labourers are few; pray ye therefore the Lord of the harvest, that he will send forth labourers into his harvest.   *Matthew 9:37–38*

When Christians answer the call to labor in God's field of harvest, they may be sent across the street to witness to a neighbor or across the ocean to a different culture. These workers must be prepared to answer a variety of questions and arguments when they confront people with the truth about heaven, hell, and eternity.

Through His Word, God has revealed Himself and given the answer to every doubt and every need in the heart of man. *How to Witness to Anyone* conveniently groups Scriptures according to topics, providing the Christian laborer with a valuable tool for ministry. The subjects and Scriptures correspond to R. A. Torrey's larger and more detailed work, *How to Bring Men to Christ*.

Study these Scriptures and prepare your heart to testify about the Lord Jesus Christ. Then, when someone with whom you are sharing the Gospel says, "I can't give up my evil ways," or, "I will lose my friends if I come to Christ," you can reply using God's own Word. Therefore, prepare yourself, and then allow God to use you in the glorious ministry of reconciliation.

You Can
Be a Soulwinner

Certain requirements must be fulfilled for real success in leading lost souls to Christ. Fortunately, these are few and simple, and anyone can meet them.

First, be a born-again believer. If you desire to bring others to Christ, you must turn away from all sin, worldliness, and selfishness, allowing Jesus to be Lord over your thoughts, purposes, and actions.

Second, truly love others and long for their salvation. If you have no love for other souls, your efforts will be mechanical and powerless. But if you, like Paul, have great heaviness and continual pain in your heart for the unsaved (Romans 9:2), the earnestness in your tone and manner will impress even the most uninterested person. Furthermore, you will be watching for opportunities to tell people about Jesus.

Third, have a working knowledge of the Bible. The Word of God is the sword of the

Spirit (Ephesians 6:17), which God uses to convict people of sin, to reveal Christ, and to regenerate the lost. You must use the Bible to bring people to Christ.

Fourth, pray frequently. Pray about whom you should speak to and what you should say. Pray that you will speak powerfully.

Fifth, be baptized in the Holy Spirit. After Jesus gave His disciples the Great Commission, He told them:

But ye shall receive power, after that the Holy Ghost is come upon you: and ye shall be witnesses unto me both in Jerusalem, and in all Judaea, and in Samaria, and unto the uttermost part of the earth.   *Acts 1:8*

The next two chapters contain promises from God's Word that explain His plan of salvation. Several chapters that follow give specific verses to answer the many objections that unbelievers have to God's plan. Then, there are chapters containing verses to help the new believer to become stronger and to weather difficult times. The final chapter gives valuable hints for you, the soulwinner.

The Promise of Salvation

1. All Have Sinned

There is no difference: for all have sinned, and come short of the glory of God.

Romans 3:22–23

If we say that we have no sin, we deceive ourselves, and the truth is not in us....If we say that we have not sinned, we make him a liar, and his word is not in us. *1 John 1:8, 10*

Thou shalt love the Lord thy God with all thy heart, and with all thy soul, and with all thy mind. This is the first and great commandment. *Matthew 22:37–38*

If thou, LORD, shouldest mark iniquities, O Lord, who shall stand? *Psalm 130:3*

2. The Consequences of Sin and Unbelief

But the wicked are like the troubled sea, when it cannot rest, whose waters cast up mire and dirt. There is no peace, saith my God, to the wicked.   *Isaiah 57:20–21*

Jesus answered them, Verily, verily, I say unto you, Whosoever committeth sin is the servant of sin.   *John 8:34*

For as many as are of the works of the law are under the curse: for it is written, Cursed is every one that continueth not in all things which are written in the book of the law to do them.   *Galatians 3:10*

He that believeth on the Son hath everlasting life: and he that believeth not the Son shall not see life; but the wrath of God abideth on him.   *John 3:36*

He that believeth on him is not condemned: but he that believeth not is condemned already, because he hath not believed in the name of the only begotten Son of God.
                     John 3:18

For the wages of sin is death; but the gift of God is eternal life through Jesus Christ our Lord.   *Romans 6:23*

The Lord Jesus shall be revealed from heaven with his mighty angels, in flaming fire taking vengeance on them that know not God, and that obey not the gospel of our Lord Jesus Christ: who shall be punished with everlasting destruction from the presence of the Lord, and from the glory of his power.

2 Thessalonians 1:7–9

Ye shall die in your sins: for if ye believe not that I am he, ye shall die in your sins.

John 8:24

But the fearful, and unbelieving, and the abominable, and murderers, and whoremongers, and sorcerers, and idolaters, and all liars, shall have their part in the lake which burneth with fire and brimstone: which is the second death.

Revelation 21:8

He that despised Moses' law died without mercy under two or three witnesses: of how much sorer punishment, suppose ye, shall he be thought worthy, who hath trodden under foot the Son of God, and hath counted the blood of the covenant, wherewith he was sanctified, an unholy thing, and hath done despite unto the Spirit of grace?

Hebrews 10:28–29

3. God's Love for Man

For God so loved the world, that he gave his only begotten Son, that whosoever believeth in him should not perish, but have everlasting life. *John 3:16*

For when we were yet without strength, in due time Christ died for the ungodly....God commendeth his love toward us, in that, while we were yet sinners, Christ died for us. *Romans 5:6, 8*

But he was wounded for our transgressions, he was bruised for our iniquities: the chastisement of our peace was upon him; and with his stripes we are healed. All we like sheep have gone astray; we have turned every one to his own way; and the LORD hath laid on him the iniquity of us all. *Isaiah 53:5–6*

And being in an agony he prayed more earnestly: and his sweat was as it were great drops of blood falling down to the ground. *Luke 22:44*

And about the ninth hour Jesus cried with a loud voice, saying, Eli, Eli, lama sabachthani?

that is to say, My God, my God, why hast thou forsaken me?   *Matthew 27:46*

Christ hath redeemed us from the curse of the law, being made a curse for us: for it is written, Cursed is every one that hangeth on a tree.   *Galatians 3:13*

Forasmuch as ye know that ye were not redeemed with corruptible things, as silver and gold, from your vain conversation received by tradition from your fathers; but with the precious blood of Christ, as of a lamb without blemish and without spot.   *1 Peter 1:18–19*

Dealing with the Openhearted

1. Jesus—Our Sin-Bearer

All we like sheep have gone astray; we have turned every one to his own way; and the LORD hath laid on him the iniquity of us all.

Isaiah 53:6

Who his own self bare our sins in his own body on the tree, that we, being dead to sins, should live unto righteousness: by whose stripes ye were healed.   *1 Peter 2:24*

Herein is love, not that we loved God, but that he loved us, and sent his Son to be the propitiation for our sins.   *1 John 4:10*

And he is the propitiation for our sins: and not for ours only, but also for the sins of the whole world.   *1 John 2:2*

For it pleased the Father that in him should all fulness dwell; and, having made peace through the blood of his cross, by him to reconcile all things unto himself; by him, I say, whether they be things in earth, or things in heaven. *Colossians 1:19–20*

In whom we have redemption through his blood, the forgiveness of sins, according to the riches of his grace. *Ephesians 1:7*

For when we were yet without strength, in due time Christ died for the ungodly. For scarcely for a righteous man will one die: yet peradventure for a good man some would even dare to die. But God commendeth his love toward us, in that, while we were yet sinners, Christ died for us. Much more then, being now justified by his blood, we shall be saved from wrath through him. For if, when we were enemies, we were reconciled to God by the death of his Son, much more, being reconciled, we shall be saved by his life. And not only so, but we also joy in God through our Lord Jesus Christ, by whom we have now received the atonement. *Romans 5:6–11*

2. Jesus—Our Risen Savior

Moreover, brethren, I declare unto you the gospel which I preached unto you, which also ye have received, and wherein ye stand; by which also ye are saved, if ye keep in memory what I preached unto you, unless ye have believed in vain. For I delivered unto you first of all that which I also received, how that Christ died for our sins according to the scriptures; and that he was buried, and that he rose again the third day according to the scriptures.

1 Corinthians 15:1–4

And she shall bring forth a son, and thou shalt call his name JESUS: for he shall save his people from their sins. *Matthew 1:21*

Now if I do that I would not, it is no more I that do it, but sin that dwelleth in me. I find then a law, that, when I would do good, evil is present with me. For I delight in the law of God after the inward man: but I see another law in my members, warring against the law of my mind, and bringing me into captivity to the law of sin which is in my members. O wretched man that I am! who shall deliver me from the body of this death? I thank God through Jesus Christ our Lord. *Romans 7:20–25*

[He] is able to keep you from falling, and to present you faultless before the presence of his glory with exceeding joy. *Jude 24*

[We] are kept by the power of God through faith unto salvation ready to be revealed in the last time.   *1 Peter 1:5*

3. Jesus—Our Ever Living Intercessor

My little children, these things write I unto you, that ye sin not. And if any man sin, we have an advocate with the Father, Jesus Christ the righteous.   *1 John 2:1*

Who is he that condemneth? It is Christ that died, yea rather, that is risen again, who is even at the right hand of God, who also maketh intercession for us.   *Romans 8:34*

Wherefore he is able also to save them to the uttermost that come unto God by him, seeing he ever liveth to make intercession for them.   *Hebrews 7:25*

4. Believing, Receiving, and Confessing Jesus

But as many as received him, to them gave he power to become the sons of God, even to them that believe on his name.   *John 1:12*

Believe on the Lord Jesus Christ, and thou shalt be saved, and thy house.   *Acts 16:31*

For God so loved the world, that he gave his only begotten Son, that whosoever believeth in him should not perish, but have everlasting life. *John 3:16*

Look unto me, and be ye saved, all the ends of the earth: for I am God, and there is none else. *Isaiah 45:22*

If thou shalt confess with thy mouth the Lord Jesus, and shalt believe in thine heart that God hath raised him from the dead, thou shalt be saved. For with the heart man believeth unto righteousness; and with the mouth confession is made unto salvation.
Romans 10:9–10

He that believeth on the Son hath everlasting life: and he that believeth not the Son shall not see life; but the wrath of God abideth on him. *John 3:36*

To him give all the prophets witness, that through his name whosoever believeth in him shall receive remission of sins. *Acts 10:43*

And by him all that believe are justified from all things, from which ye could not be justified by the law of Moses. *Acts 13:39*

Dealing with Difficulties

1. I am too great a sinner.

This is a faithful saying, and worthy of all acceptation, that Christ Jesus came into the world to save sinners; of whom I am chief.

1 Timothy 1:15

For when we were yet without strength, in due time Christ died for the ungodly....God commendeth his love toward us, in that, while we were yet sinners, Christ died for us.

Romans 5:6, 8

Come now, and let us reason together, saith the LORD: though your sins be as scarlet, they shall be as white as snow; though they be red like crimson, they shall be as wool.

Isaiah 1:18

To him give all the prophets witness, that through his name whosoever believeth in him shall receive remission of sins.   *Acts 10:43*

For the Son of man is come to seek and to save that which was lost. *Luke 19:10*

All that the Father giveth me shall come to me; and him that cometh to me I will in no wise cast out. *John 6:37*

2. I am afraid of failure.

And I give unto them eternal life; and they shall never perish, neither shall any man pluck them out of my hand. My Father, which gave them me, is greater than all; and no man is able to pluck them out of my Father's hand.
John 10:28–29

Fear thou not; for I am with thee: be not dismayed; for I am thy God: I will strengthen thee; yea, I will help thee; yea, I will uphold thee with the right hand of my righteousness....For I the LORD thy God will hold thy right hand, saying unto thee, Fear not; I will help thee. *Isaiah 41:10, 13*

[We] are kept by the power of God through faith unto salvation ready to be revealed in the last time. *1 Peter 1:5*

For the which cause I also suffer these things: nevertheless I am not ashamed: for I know whom I have believed, and am persuaded that he is able to keep that which I have committed unto him against that day.

2 Timothy 1:12

Be strong and courageous, be not afraid nor dismayed for the king of Assyria, nor for all the multitude that is with him: for there be more with us than with him: with him is an arm of flesh; but with us is the LORD our God to help us, and to fight our battles.

2 Chronicles 32:7–8

Who art thou that judgest another man's servant? to his own master he standeth or falleth. Yea, he shall be holden up: for God is able to make him stand.   *Romans 14:4*

But the Lord is faithful, who shall stablish you, and keep you from evil.

2 Thessalonians 3:3

There hath no temptation taken you but such as is common to man: but God is faithful, who will not suffer you to be tempted above that ye are able; but will with the temptation also make a way to escape, that ye may be able to bear it.   *1 Corinthians 10:13*

3. I am too weak.

And he said unto me, My grace is sufficient for thee: for my strength is made perfect in weakness. Most gladly therefore will I rather glory in my infirmities, that the power of Christ may rest upon me. Therefore I take pleasure in infirmities, in reproaches, in necessities, in persecutions, in distresses for Christ's sake: for when I am weak, then am I strong.
2 Corinthians 12:9–10

I can do all things through Christ which strengtheneth me. *Philippians 4:13*

For what the law could not do, in that it was weak through the flesh, God sending his own Son in the likeness of sinful flesh, and for sin, condemned sin in the flesh: that the righteousness of the law might be fulfilled in us, who walk not after the flesh, but after the Spirit. *Romans 8:3–4*

He giveth power to the faint; and to them that have no might he increaseth strength. Even the youths shall faint and be weary, and the young men shall utterly fall: but they that wait upon the LORD shall renew their strength; they shall mount up with wings as

eagles; they shall run, and not be weary; and
they shall walk, and not faint.

Isaiah 40:29–31

Thy word have I hid in mine heart, that I
might not sin against thee. *Psalm 119:11*

For whatsoever is born of God overcometh
the world: and this is the victory that overcometh the world, even our faith. *1 John 5:4*

Be sober, be vigilant; because your adversary the devil, as a roaring lion, walketh about,
seeking whom he may devour: whom resist
stedfast in the faith, knowing that the same
afflictions are accomplished in your brethren
that are in the world. But the God of all grace,
who hath called us unto his eternal glory by
Christ Jesus, after that ye have suffered a
while, make you perfect, stablish, strengthen,
settle you. *1 Peter 5:8–10*

4. I can't give up my evil ways and bad habits.

Be not deceived; God is not mocked: for
whatsoever a man soweth, that shall he also
reap. For he that soweth to his flesh shall of
the flesh reap corruption; but he that soweth

to the Spirit shall of the Spirit reap life ever-lasting. *Galatians 6:7–8*

I can do all things through Christ which strengtheneth me. *Philippians 4:13*

If the Son therefore shall make you free, ye shall be free indeed. *John 8:36*

5. I will be persecuted if I become a Christian.

Yea, and all that will live godly in Christ Jesus shall suffer persecution. *2 Timothy 3:12*

Blessed are they which are persecuted for righteousness' sake: for theirs is the kingdom of heaven. Blessed are ye, when men shall revile you, and persecute you, and shall say all manner of evil against you falsely, for my sake. Rejoice, and be exceeding glad: for great is your reward in heaven: for so persecuted they the prophets which were before you.

Matthew 5:10–12

For whosoever will save his life shall lose it; but whosoever shall lose his life for my sake and the gospel's, the same shall save it....Whosoever therefore shall be ashamed of me and of my words in this adulterous and sinful generation; of him also shall the Son of man be ashamed, when he cometh in the glory of his Father with the holy angels.

Mark 8:35, 38

For I reckon that the sufferings of this present time are not worthy to be compared with the glory which shall be revealed in us.

Romans 8:18

Continue in the faith...[for] we must through much tribulation enter into the kingdom of God.

Acts 14:22

And when they had called the apostles, and beaten them, they commanded that they should not speak in the name of Jesus, and let them go. And they departed from the presence of the council, rejoicing that they were counted worthy to suffer shame for his name.

Acts 5:40–41

If we suffer, we shall also reign with him: if we deny him, he also will deny us.

2 Timothy 2:12

Looking unto Jesus the author and finisher of our faith; who for the joy that was set before him endured the cross, despising the shame, and is set down at the right hand of the throne of God. For consider him that endured such contradiction of sinners against himself, lest ye be wearied and faint in your minds.

Hebrews 12:2–3

For what glory is it, if, when ye be buffeted for your faults, ye shall take it patiently? but if, when ye do well, and suffer for it, ye take it patiently, this is acceptable with God. For even hereunto were ye called: because Christ also suffered for us, leaving us an example, that ye should follow his steps.

1 Peter 2:20–21

6. I will lose my friends.

The fear of man bringeth a snare: but whoso putteth his trust in the LORD shall be safe. *Proverbs 29:25*

He that walketh with wise men shall be wise: but a companion of fools shall be destroyed. *Proverbs 13:20*

Blessed is the man that walketh not in the counsel of the ungodly, nor standeth in the way of sinners, nor sitteth in the seat of the scornful. But his delight is in the law of the LORD; and in his law doth he meditate day and night. *Psalm 1:1-2*

That which we have seen and heard declare we unto you, that ye also may have fellowship with us: and truly our fellowship is with the Father, and with his Son Jesus Christ. *1 John 1:3*

Ye adulterers and adulteresses, know ye not that the friendship of the world is enmity with God? whosoever therefore will be a friend of the world is the enemy of God. *James 4:4*

7. I have too much to give up.

For what shall it profit a man, if he shall gain the whole world, and lose his own soul? *Mark 8:36*

But seek ye first the kingdom of God, and his righteousness; and all these things shall be added unto you. *Matthew 6:33*

For the LORD God is a sun and shield: the LORD will give grace and glory: no good thing will he withhold from them that walk uprightly. *Psalm 84:11*

He that spared not his own Son, but delivered him up for us all, how shall he not with him also freely give us all things? *Romans 8:32*

Love not the world, neither the things that are in the world. If any man love the world, the love of the Father is not in him. For all that is in the world, the lust of the flesh, and the lust of the eyes, and the pride of life, is not of the Father, but is of the world. And the world passeth away, and the lust thereof: but he that doeth the will of God abideth for ever.
1 John 2:15–17

By faith Moses, when he was come to years, refused to be called the son of Pharaoh's daughter; choosing rather to suffer affliction with the people of God, than to enjoy the pleasures of sin for a season; esteeming the reproach of Christ greater riches than the treasures in Egypt: for he had respect unto the recompense of the reward. *Hebrews 11:24–26*

But what things were gain to me, those I counted loss for Christ. Yea doubtless, and I count all things but loss for the excellency of the knowledge of Christ Jesus my Lord: for whom I have suffered the loss of all things, and do count them but dung, that I may win Christ. *Philippians 3:7–8*

The ground of a certain rich man brought forth plentifully: and he thought within himself, saying, What shall I do, because I have no room where to bestow my fruits? And he said, This will I do: I will pull down my barns, and build greater; and there will I bestow all my fruits and my goods. And I will say to my soul, Soul, thou hast much goods laid up for many years; take thine ease, eat, drink, and be merry. But God said unto him, Thou fool, this night thy soul shall be required of thee: then whose shall those things be, which thou hast provided? So is he that layeth up treasure for himself, and is not rich toward God.

Luke 12:16–21

For my yoke is easy, and my burden is light. *Matthew 11:30*

8. I don't have the right feelings.

God does not demand that we feel sorry for our sins, but that we turn from sin and receive Christ.

For with the heart man believeth unto righteousness; and with the mouth confession is made unto salvation. *Romans 10:10*

33

Let the wicked forsake his way, and the unrighteous man his thoughts: and let him return unto the LORD, and he will have mercy upon him; and to our God, for he will abundantly pardon. *Isaiah 55:7*

But as many as received him, to them gave he power to become the sons of God, even to them that believe on his name. *John 1:12*

Believe on the Lord Jesus Christ, and thou shalt be saved, and thy house. *Acts 16:31*

9. I am seeking Christ but cannot find Him.

And ye shall seek me, and find me, when ye shall search for me with all your heart.
Jeremiah 29:13

What man of you, having an hundred sheep, if he lose one of them, doth not leave the ninety and nine in the wilderness, and go after that which is lost, until he find it? And when he hath found it, he layeth it on his shoulders, rejoicing. And when he cometh home, he calleth together his friends and neighbours, saying unto them, Rejoice with me; for I have found my sheep which was lost. I say unto you, that likewise joy shall be in heaven over one sinner that repenteth, more than over ninety and nine just persons, which need no repentance. Either what woman having ten pieces of silver, if she lose one piece, doth not light a candle, and sweep the house, and seek diligently till she find it? And when she hath found it, she calleth her friends and her neighbours together, saying, Rejoice with me; for I have found the piece which I had lost. Likewise, I say unto you, there is joy in the presence of the angels of God over one sinner that repenteth. *Luke 15:4–10*

For the Son of man is come to seek and to save that which was lost. *Luke 19:10*

Also read the passages under Jesus—Our Sin-Bearer.

10. My heart is too hard.

A new heart also will I give you, and a new spirit will I put within you: and I will take away the stony heart out of your flesh, and I will give you an heart of flesh. And I will put my spirit within you, and cause you to walk in my statutes, and ye shall keep my judgments, and do them. *Ezekiel 36:26–27*

11. God will not receive me.

All that the Father giveth me shall come to me; and him that cometh to me I will in no wise cast out.   *John 6:37*

For whosoever shall call upon the name of the Lord shall be saved.   *Romans 10:13*

Manasseh was twelve years old when he began to reign, and he reigned fifty and five years in Jerusalem: but did that which was evil in the sight of the LORD, like unto the abominations of the heathen, whom the LORD had cast out before the children of Israel....And the LORD spake to Manasseh, and to his people: but they would not hearken. Wherefore the LORD brought upon them the captains of the host of the king of Assyria, which took Manasseh among the thorns, and bound him with fetters, and carried him to Babylon. And when he was in affliction, he besought the LORD his God, and humbled himself greatly before the God of his fathers, and prayed unto him: and he was entreated of him, and heard his supplication, and brought him again to Jerusalem into his kingdom. Then Manasseh knew that the LORD he was God.
                    2 Chronicles 33:1–2, 10–13

12. I have committed the unpardonable sin.

What is the unpardonable sin?

Wherefore I say unto you, All manner of sin and blasphemy shall be forgiven unto men: but the blasphemy against the Holy Ghost shall not be forgiven unto men. And whosoever speaketh a word against the Son of man, it shall be forgiven him: but whosoever speaketh against the Holy Ghost, it shall not be forgiven him, neither in this world, neither in the world to come. *Matthew 12:31–32*

For it is impossible for those who were once enlightened, and have tasted of the heavenly gift, and were made partakers of the Holy Ghost, and have tasted the good word of God, and the powers of the world to come, if they shall fall away, to renew them again unto repentance; seeing they crucify to themselves the Son of God afresh, and put him to an open shame. *Hebrews 6:4–6*

This passage describes one who renounces Christianity and returns to the things of this world, not one who merely falls into sin, even deep sin, as Peter did.

13. It is too late.

When thou art in tribulation, and all these things are come upon thee, even in the latter days, if thou turn to the LORD thy God, and shalt be obedient unto his voice; (for the LORD thy God is a merciful God;) he will not forsake thee, neither destroy thee, nor forget the covenant of thy fathers which he sware unto them.
Deuteronomy 4:30–31

The Lord is not slack concerning his promise, as some men count slackness; but is longsuffering to us-ward, not willing that any should perish, but that all should come to repentance.
2 Peter 3:9

And the Spirit and the bride say, Come. And let him that heareth say, Come. And let him that is athirst come. And whosoever will, let him take the water of life freely.
Revelation 22:17

14. I must become a better person first.

They that be whole need not a physician, but they that are sick. But go ye and learn what that meaneth, I will have mercy, and not sacrifice: for I am not come to call the right-eous, but sinners to repentance.

Matthew 9:12–13

I will arise and go to my father, and will say unto him, Father, I have sinned against heaven, and before thee....And he arose, and came to his father. But when he was yet a great way off, his father saw him, and had compassion, and ran, and fell on his neck, and kissed him. And the son said unto him, Father, I have sinned against heaven, and in thy sight, and am no more worthy to be called thy son. But the father said to his servants, Bring forth the best robe, and put it on him; and put a ring on his hand, and shoes on his feet: and bring hither the fatted calf, and kill it; and let us eat, and be merry: for this my son was dead, and is alive again; he was lost, and is found.

Luke 15:18, 20–24

Two men went up into the temple to pray; the one a Pharisee, and the other a publican. The Pharisee stood and prayed thus with him-self, God, I thank thee, that I am not as other men are, extortioners, unjust, adulterers, or even as this publican. I fast twice in the week, I give tithes of all that I possess. And the pub-lican, standing afar off, would not lift up so much as his eyes unto heaven, but smote upon his breast, saying, God be merciful to me a sinner. I tell you, this man went down to his house justified rather than the other: for every one that exalteth himself shall be abased; and he that humbleth himself shall be exalted.

Luke 18:10–14

I have blotted out, as a thick cloud, thy transgressions, and, as a cloud, thy sins: return unto me; for I have redeemed thee.

Isaiah 44:22

Dealing with the Self-Righteous

1. I'm no worse than anybody else.

Knowing that a man is not justified by the works of the law, but by the faith of Jesus Christ, even we have believed in Jesus Christ, that we might be justified by the faith of Christ, and not by the works of the law: for by the works of the law shall no flesh be justified.
Galatians 2:16

Now we know that what things soever the law saith, it saith to them who are under the law: that every mouth may be stopped, and all the world may become guilty before God. Therefore by the deeds of the law there shall no flesh be justified in his sight: for by the law is the knowledge of sin.   *Romans 3:19–20*

For as many as are of the works of the law are under the curse: for it is written, Cursed is every one that continueth not in all things which are written in the book of the law to do them. *Galatians 3:10*

For whosoever shall keep the whole law, and yet offend in one point, he is guilty of all. *James 2:10*

Except your righteousness shall exceed the righteousness of the scribes and Pharisees, ye shall in no case enter into the kingdom of heaven. *Matthew 5:20*

And he said unto them, Ye are they which justify yourselves before men; but God knoweth your hearts: for that which is highly esteemed among men is abomination in the sight of God. *Luke 16:15*

God shall judge the secrets of men by Jesus Christ according to my gospel. *Romans 2:16*

Man looketh on the outward appearance, but the LORD looketh on the heart. *1 Samuel 16:7*

But without faith it is impossible to please him: for he that cometh to God must believe

that he is, and that he is a rewarder of them
that diligently seek him.   *Hebrews 11:6*

He that despised Moses' law died without
mercy under two or three witnesses: of how
much sorer punishment, suppose ye, shall he
be thought worthy, who hath trodden under
foot the Son of God, and hath counted the
blood of the covenant, wherewith he was sanctified, an unholy thing, and hath done despite
unto the Spirit of grace?   *Hebrews 10:28–29*

2. God is too good to damn anyone.

Or despisest thou the riches of his goodness and forbearance and longsuffering; not
knowing that the goodness of God leadeth thee
to repentance? But after thy hardness and impenitent heart treasurest up unto thyself
wrath against the day of wrath and revelation
of the righteous judgment of God.

Romans 2:4–5

If ye believe not that I am he, ye shall die
in your sins.   *John 8:24*

The Lord is not slack concerning his
promise, as some men count slackness; but is
longsuffering to us-ward, not willing that any

should perish, but that all should come to repentance. But the day of the Lord will come as a thief in the night; in the which the heavens shall pass away with a great noise, and the elements shall melt with fervent heat, the earth also and the works that are therein shall be burned up. Seeing then that all these things shall be dissolved, what manner of persons ought ye to be in all holy conversation and godliness? *2 Peter 3:9–11*

I have no pleasure in the death of the wicked; but that the wicked turn from his way and live: turn ye, turn ye from your evil ways; for why will ye die, O house of Israel?
Ezekiel 33:11

For if God spared not the angels that sinned, but cast them down to hell, and delivered them into chains of darkness, to be reserved unto judgment; and spared not the old world, but saved Noah the eighth person, a preacher of righteousness, bringing in the flood upon the world of the ungodly; and turning the cities of Sodom and Gomorrha into ashes condemned them with an overthrow, making them an ensample unto those that after should live ungodly...the Lord knoweth how to deliver the godly out of temptations, and to reserve the unjust unto the day of judgment to be punished.   *2 Peter 2:4–6, 9*

Except ye repent, ye shall all likewise perish.   *Luke 13:3*

He that believeth on him is not condemned: but he that believeth not is condemned already, because he hath not believed in the name of the only begotten Son of God.
                                        John 3:18

3. I'm trying to be a good Christian.

We are saved by trusting what Jesus has done and will do, not by any effort of our own.

For all have sinned, and come short of the glory of God; being justified freely by his grace through the redemption that is in Christ Jesus: whom God hath set forth to be a propitiation through faith in his blood.
                                        Romans 3:23–25

For what saith the scripture? Abraham believed God, and it was counted unto him for righteousness. Now to him that worketh is the reward not reckoned of grace, but of debt. But to him that worketh not, but believeth on him that justified the ungodly, his faith is counted for righteousness.   *Romans 4:3–5*

But as many as received him, to them gave he power to become the sons of God, even to them that believe on his name.   *John 1:12*

Behold, God is my salvation; I will trust, and not be afraid: for the LORD JEHOVAH is my strength and my song; he also is become my salvation.   *Isaiah 12:2*

4. I feel that I am saved.

There is a way which seemeth right unto a man, but the end thereof are the ways of death.   *Proverbs 14:12*

He that believeth on the Son hath everlasting life: and he that believeth not the Son shall not see life; but the wrath of God abideth on him.   *John 3:36*

5. I belong to a church.

Follow peace with all men, and holiness, without which no man shall see the Lord.
                    Hebrews 12:14

Know ye not that the unrighteous shall not inherit the kingdom of God? Be not deceived: neither fornicators, nor idolaters, nor adulterers, nor effeminate, nor abusers of themselves with mankind, nor thieves, nor covetous, nor drunkards, nor revilers, nor extortioners, shall inherit the kingdom of God.

1 Corinthians 6:9–10

They profess that they know God; but in works they deny him, being abominable, and disobedient, and unto every good work reprobate.

Titus 1:16

What doth it profit, my brethren, though a man say he hath faith, and have not works? can faith save him?

James 2:14

Jesus answered and said unto him, Verily, verily, I say unto thee, Except a man be born again, he cannot see the kingdom of God.

John 3:3

If ye know that he is righteous, ye know that every one that doeth righteousness is born of him.

1 John 2:29

But the fearful, and unbelieving, and the abominable, and murderers, and whoremongers,

47

and sorcerers, and idolaters, and all liars, shall
have their part in the lake which burneth with
fire and brimstone: which is the second death.

Revelation 21:8

Dealing with the Uncertain and with Backsliders

1. How can I know I am saved?

These things have I written unto you that believe on the name of the Son of God; that ye may know that ye have eternal life.

1 John 5:13

Verily, verily, I say unto you, He that heareth my word, and believeth on him that sent me, hath everlasting life, and shall not come into condemnation; but is passed from death unto life. *John 5:24*

And this is the record, that God hath given to us eternal life, and this life is in his Son. He that hath the Son hath life; and he that hath not the Son of God hath not life.

1 John 5:11–12

I am the light of the world: he that fol-
loweth me shall not walk in darkness, but shall
have the light of life.   *John 8:12*

Let the wicked forsake his way, and the
unrighteous man his thoughts: and let him return unto the LORD, and he will have mercy
upon him; and to our God, for he will abundantly pardon.   *Isaiah 55:7*

2. I don't care about serving God anymore.

What iniquity have your fathers found in
me, that they are gone far from me, and have
walked after vanity, and are become vain?...
For my people have committed two evils; they
have forsaken me the fountain of living waters,
and hewed them out cisterns, broken cisterns,
that can hold no water....Thine own wicked-
ness shall correct thee, and thy backslidings
shall reprove thee: know therefore and see that
it is an evil thing and bitter, that thou hast
forsaken the LORD thy God, and that my fear
is not in thee, saith the Lord GOD of hosts.
             Jeremiah 2:5, 13, 19

I have overthrown some of you, as God
overthrew Sodom and Gomorrah, and ye were
as a firebrand plucked out of the burning: yet

have ye not returned unto me, saith the LORD. Therefore thus will I do unto thee, O Israel: and because I will do this unto thee, prepare to meet thy God, O Israel.   *Amos 4:11–12*

The backslider in heart shall be filled with his own ways: and a good man shall be satisfied from himself.   *Proverbs 14:14*

3. I want to come back to the Lord.

Go and proclaim these words toward the north, and say, Return, thou backsliding Israel, saith the LORD; and I will not cause mine anger to fall upon you: for I am merciful, saith the LORD, and I will not keep anger for ever. Only acknowledge thine iniquity, that thou hast transgressed against the LORD thy God, and hast scattered thy ways to the strangers under every green tree, and ye have not obeyed my voice, saith the LORD....Return, ye backsliding children, and I will heal your backslidings. Behold, we come unto thee; for thou art the LORD our God.   *Jeremiah 3:12–13, 22*

O Israel, return unto the LORD thy God; for thou hast fallen by thine iniquity. Take with you words, and turn to the LORD: say unto him, Take away all iniquity, and receive us graciously: so will we render the calves of our lips. Asshur shall not save us; we will not ride upon horses: neither will we say any more to the work of our hands, Ye are our gods: for in thee the fatherless findeth mercy. I will heal their backsliding, I will love them freely: for mine anger is turned away from him.

Hosea 14:1–4

But thou hast not called upon me, O Jacob; but thou hast been weary of me, O Israel....Thou hast bought me no sweet cane with money, neither hast thou filled me with the fat of thy sacrifices: but thou hast made me to serve with thy sins, thou hast wearied me with thine iniquities. I, even I, am he that blotteth out thy transgressions for mine own sake, and will not remember thy sins.

Isaiah 43:22, 24–25

I have blotted out, as a thick cloud, thy transgressions, and, as a cloud, thy sins: return unto me; for I have redeemed thee.

Isaiah 44:22

For I know the thoughts that I think toward you, saith the LORD, thoughts of peace, and not of evil, to give you an expected end. Then shall ye call upon me, and ye shall go and pray unto me, and I will hearken unto you.

And ye shall seek me, and find me, when ye shall search for me with all your heart.

Jeremiah 29:11–13

And there ye shall serve gods, the work of men's hands, wood and stone, which neither see, nor hear, nor eat, nor smell. But if from thence thou shalt seek the LORD thy God, thou shalt find him, if thou seek him with all thy heart and with all thy soul. When thou art in tribulation, and all these things are come upon thee, even in the latter days, if thou turn to the LORD thy God, and shalt be obedient unto his voice; (for the LORD thy God is a merciful God;) he will not forsake thee, neither destroy thee, nor forget the covenant of thy fathers which he sware unto them.

Deuteronomy 4:28–31

If my people, which are called by my name, shall humble themselves, and pray, and seek my face, and turn from their wicked ways; then will I hear from heaven, and will forgive their sin, and will heal their land.

2 Chronicles 7:14

If we confess our sins, he is faithful and just to forgive us our sins, and to cleanse us from all unrighteousness. *1 John 1:9*

But when they in their trouble did turn unto the LORD God of Israel, and sought him, he was found of them.   *2 Chronicles 15:4*

And not many days after the younger son gathered all together, and took his journey into a far country, and there wasted his substance with riotous living. And when he had spent all, there arose a mighty famine in that land; and he began to be in want. And he went and joined himself to a citizen of that country; and he sent him into his fields to feed swine. And he would fain have filled his belly with the husks that the swine did eat: and no man gave unto him. And when he came to himself, he said, How many hired servants of my father's have bread enough and to spare, and I perish with hunger! I will arise and go to my father, and will say unto him, Father, I have sinned against heaven, and before thee, and am no more worthy to be called thy son: make me as one of thy hired servants. And he arose, and came to his father. But when he was yet a great way off, his father saw him, and had compassion, and ran, and fell on his neck, and kissed him. And the son said unto him, Father, I have sinned against heaven, and in thy sight, and am no more worthy to be called thy son. But the father said to his servants, Bring forth the best robe, and put it on him; and put a ring on his hand, and shoes on his feet: and bring hither the fatted calf, and kill it; and let us eat, and be merry: for this my son was dead, and is alive again; he was lost, and is found. And they began to be merry. *Luke 15:13–24*

Dealing with Skeptics

1. The Bible and God's plan of salvation seem foolish to me.

For the preaching of the cross is to them that perish foolishness; but unto us which are saved it is the power of God.

1 Corinthians 1:18

But if our gospel be hid, it is hid to them that are lost: in whom the god of this world hath blinded the minds of them which believe not, lest the light of the glorious gospel of Christ, who is the image of God, should shine unto them.

2 Corinthians 4:3–4

The Lord Jesus shall be revealed from heaven with his mighty angels, in flaming fire taking vengeance on them that know not God, and that obey not the gospel of our Lord Jesus Christ.

2 Thessalonians 1:7–8

Then shall that Wicked be revealed...even him, whose coming is after the working of Satan with all power and signs and lying wonders, and with all deceivableness of unrighteousness in them that perish; because they received not the love of the truth, that they might be saved. And for this cause God shall send them strong delusion, that they should believe a lie: that they all might be damned who believed not the truth, but had pleasure in unrighteousness.

2 Thessalonians 2:8–12

He that believeth and is baptized shall be saved; but he that believeth not shall be damned. *Mark 16:16*

2. I've tried, but I can't believe.

If any man will do his will, he shall know of the doctrine, whether it be of God, or whether I speak of myself. *John 7:17*

But the natural man receiveth not the things of the Spirit of God: for they are foolishness unto him: neither can he know them, because they are spiritually discerned.

1 Corinthians 2:14

Philip findeth Nathanael, and saith unto him, We have found him, of whom Moses in the law, and the prophets, did write, Jesus of Nazareth, the son of Joseph. And Nathanael

57

said unto him, Can there any good thing come out of Nazareth? Philip saith unto him, Come and see. Jesus saw Nathanael coming to him, and saith of him, Behold an Israelite indeed, in whom is no guile! Nathanael saith unto him, Whence knowest thou me? Jesus answered and said unto him, Before that Philip called thee, when thou wast under the fig tree, I saw thee. Nathanael answered and saith unto him, Rabbi, thou art the Son of God; thou art the King of Israel. *John 1:45–49*

But Thomas, one of the twelve, called Didymus, was not with them when Jesus came. The other disciples therefore said unto him, We have seen the Lord. But he said unto them, Except I shall see in his hands the print of the nails, and put my finger into the print of the nails, and thrust my hand into his side, I will not believe. And after eight days again his disciples were within, and Thomas with them: then came Jesus, the doors being shut, and stood in the midst, and said, Peace be unto you. Then saith he to Thomas, Reach hither thy finger, and behold my hands; and reach hither thy hand, and thrust it into my side: and be not faithless, but believing. And Thomas answered and said unto him, My Lord and my God. Jesus saith unto him, Thomas, because thou hast seen me, thou hast believed:

blessed are they that have not seen, and yet have believed.   *John 20:24–29*

The officers answered, Never man spake like this man.   *John 7:46*

Have I been so long time with you, and yet hast thou not known me, Philip? he that hath seen me hath seen the Father; and how sayest thou then, Show us the Father? Believest thou not that I am in the Father, and the Father in me? the words that I speak unto you I speak not of myself: but the Father that dwelleth in me, he doeth the works. Believe me that I am in the Father, and the Father in me: or else believe for the very works' sake. *John 14:9–11*

If I had not done among them the works which none other man did, they had not had sin: but now have they both seen and hated both me and my Father.   *John 15:24*

He that is of God heareth God's words: ye therefore hear them not, because ye are not of God.   *John 8:47*

For God sent not his Son into the world to condemn the world; but that the world through him might be saved. He that believeth on him is not condemned: but he that believeth not is condemned already, because he hath not believed in the name of the only begotten Son of God. And this is the condemnation, that light is come into the world, and men loved darkness rather than light, because their deeds were evil. For every one that doeth evil hateth the light, neither cometh to the light, lest his deeds should be reproved. But he that doeth truth cometh to the light, that his deeds may be made manifest, that they are wrought in God. *John 3:17–21*

And many other signs truly did Jesus in the presence of his disciples, which are not written in this book: but these are written, that ye might believe that Jesus is the Christ, the Son of God; and that believing ye might have life through his name. *John 20:30–31*

3. I don't believe there is a God.

That which may be known of God is manifest in them; for God hath showed it unto them. For the invisible things of him from the creation of the world are clearly seen, being understood by the things that are made, even his eternal power and Godhead; so that they are without excuse: because that, when they knew God, they glorified him not as God, neither were thankful; but became vain in their imaginations, and their foolish heart was darkened. Professing themselves to be wise, they became fools.   *Romans 1:19–22*

The heavens declare the glory of God; and the firmament showeth his handiwork.
                                        Psalm 19:1

The fool hath said in his heart, There is no God. They are corrupt, they have done abominable works, there is none that doeth good.
                                        Psalm 14:1

4. Is the Bible the Word of God?

[You make] the word of God of none effect through your tradition, which ye have delivered: and many such like things do ye.
                                        Mark 7:13

Heaven and earth shall pass away, but my words shall not pass away.   *Matthew 24:35*

Till heaven and earth pass, one jot or one tittle shall in no wise pass from the law, till all be fulfilled.   *Matthew 5:18*

Beginning at Moses and all the prophets, he expounded unto them in all the scriptures the things concerning himself....And he said unto them, These are the words which I spake unto you, while I was yet with you, that all things must be fulfilled, which were written in the law of Moses, and in the prophets, and in the psalms, concerning me.   *Luke 24:27, 44*

For this cause also thank we God without ceasing, because, when ye received the word of God which ye heard of us, ye received it not as the word of men, but as it is in truth, the word of God, which effectually worketh also in you that believe.   *1 Thessalonians 2:13*

We have also a more sure word of prophecy; whereunto ye do well that ye take heed, as unto a light that shineth in a dark place, until the day dawn, and the day star arise in your hearts: knowing this first, that no prophecy of the scripture is of any private interpretation. For the prophecy came not in old time by the will of man: but holy men of God spake as they were moved by the Holy Ghost.

2 Peter 1:19–21

He that believeth on the Son of God hath the witness in himself: he that believeth not God hath made him a liar; because he believeth not the record that God gave of his Son.

1 John 5:10

He that is of God heareth God's words: ye therefore hear them not, because ye are not of God.   *John 8:47*

5. Is Jesus the Son of God?

The word which God sent unto the children of Israel, preaching peace by Jesus Christ: (he is Lord of all:) that word, I say, ye know.
                                         Acts 10:36–37

But we speak the wisdom of God in a mystery, even the hidden wisdom, which God ordained before the world unto our glory: which none of the princes of this world knew: for had they known it, they would not have crucified the Lord of glory.   *1 Corinthians 2:7–8*

But unto the Son he saith, Thy throne, O God, is for ever and ever: a sceptre of righteousness is the sceptre of thy kingdom.
                                           Hebrews 1:8

And Thomas answered and said unto him, My Lord and my God. Jesus saith unto him, Thomas, because thou hast seen me, thou hast believed: blessed are they that have not seen, and yet have believed.   *John 20:28–29*

But these are written, that ye might believe that Jesus is the Christ, the Son of God; and that believing ye might have life through his name. *John 20:31*

All men should honour the Son, even as they honour the Father. He that honoureth not the Son honoureth not the Father which hath sent him. *John 5:23*

Wherefore God also hath highly exalted him, and given him a name which is above every name: that at the name of Jesus every knee should bow, of things in heaven, and things in earth, and things under the earth.
Philippians 2:9–10

Who is a liar but he that denieth that Jesus is the Christ? He is antichrist, that denieth the Father and the Son. Whosoever denieth the Son, the same hath not the Father: (but) he that acknowledgeth the Son hath the Father also. *1 John 2:22–23*

Whosoever believeth that Jesus is the Christ is born of God: and every one that loveth him that begat loveth him also that is begotten of him....Who is he that overcometh

the world, but he that believeth that Jesus is
the Son of God?   *1 John 5:1, 5*

Ye shall die in your sins: for if ye believe
not that I am he, ye shall die in your sins.
                                   John 8:24

Dealing with Objections

1. God is unjust and cruel to create men and then damn them.

Nay but, O man, who art thou that repliest against God? Shall the thing formed say to him that formed it, Why hast thou made me thus?
Romans 9:20

For my thoughts are not your thoughts, neither are your ways my ways, saith the LORD. For as the heavens are higher than the earth, so are my ways higher than your ways, and my thoughts than your thoughts.
Isaiah 55:8–9

Shall he that contendeth with the Almighty instruct him? he that reproveth God, let him answer it.
Job 40:2

My son, despise not thou the chastening of the Lord, nor faint when thou art rebuked of him: for whom the Lord loveth he chasteneth, and scourgeth every son whom he receiveth.... Now no chastening for the present seemeth to be joyous, but grievous: nevertheless afterward it yieldeth the peaceable fruit of righteousness unto them which are exercised thereby.

Hebrews 12:5–6, 11

2. The Bible has too many contradictions, and I can't understand it.

But the natural man receiveth not the things of the Spirit of God: for they are foolishness unto him: neither can he know them, because they are spiritually discerned.

1 Corinthians 2:14

O the depth of the riches both of the wisdom and knowledge of God! how unsearchable are his judgments, and his ways past finding out! *Romans 11:33*

When I was a child, I spake as a child, I understood as a child, I thought as a child: but when I became a man, I put away childish things. For now we see through a glass, darkly; but then face to face: now I know in part; but then shall I know even as also I am known.

1 Corinthians 13:11–12

Open thou mine eyes, that I may behold wondrous things out of thy law.   *Psalm 119:18*

In all his epistles, [Paul spoke] in them of these things; in which are some things hard to be understood, which they that are unlearned and unstable wrest, as they do also the other scriptures, unto their own destruction. Ye therefore, beloved, seeing ye know these things before, beware lest ye also, being led away with the error of the wicked, fall from your own stedfastness. But grow in grace, and in the knowledge of our Lord and Saviour Jesus Christ. To him be glory both now and for ever. Amen.   *2 Peter 3:16–18*

3. There are too many hypocrites in church.

So then every one of us shall give account of himself to God.   *Romans 14:12*

Therefore thou art inexcusable, O man, whosoever thou art that judgest: for wherein thou judgest another, thou condemnest thyself; for thou that judgest doest the same things. But we are sure that the judgment of God is according to truth against them which commit such things. And thinkest thou this, O man, that judgest them which do such things, and doest the same, that thou shalt escape the judgment of God? Or despisest thou the riches of his goodness and forbearance and longsuffering; not knowing that the goodness of God leadeth thee to repentance? But after thy hardness and impenitent heart treasurest up unto thyself wrath against the day of wrath and revelation of the righteous judgment of God.   *Romans 2:1–5*

Judge not, that ye be not judged. For with what judgment ye judge, ye shall be judged; and with what measure ye mete, it shall be measured to you again. And why beholdest thou the mote that is in thy brother's eye, but considerest not the beam that is in thine own eye? Or how wilt thou say to thy brother, Let me pull out the mote out of thine eye; and, behold, a beam is in thine own eye? Thou hypocrite, first cast out the beam out of thine own eye; and then shalt thou see clearly to cast out the mote out of thy brother's eye.

Matthew 7:1–5

4. I'll accept Christ some time in the future.

Seek ye the LORD while he may be found, call ye upon him while he is near.   *Isaiah 55:6*

Boast not thyself of to morrow; for thou knowest not what a day may bring forth.

Proverbs 27:1

He, that being often reproved hardeneth his neck, shall suddenly be destroyed, and that without remedy.

Proverbs 29:1

Therefore be ye also ready: for in such an hour as ye think not the Son of man cometh.

Matthew 24:44

And while they went to buy, the bridegroom came; and they that were ready went in with him to the marriage: and the door was shut. Afterward came also the other virgins, saying, Lord, Lord, open to us. But he answered and said, Verily I say unto you, I know you not. Watch therefore, for ye know neither the day nor the hour wherein the Son of man cometh.

Matthew 25:10–13

And I will say to my soul, Soul, thou hast much goods laid up for many years; take thine ease, eat, drink, and be merry. But God said unto him, Thou fool, this night thy soul shall be required of thee: then whose shall those things be, which thou hast provided?

Luke 12:19–20

And Elijah came unto all the people, and said, How long halt ye between two opinions? if the LORD be God, follow him: but if Baal, then follow him. *1 Kings 18:21*

Go to now, ye that say, To day or to morrow we will go into such a city, and continue there a year, and buy and sell, and get gain: whereas ye know not what shall be on the morrow. For what is your life? It is even a vapour, that appeareth for a little time, and then vanisheth away. *James 4:13–14*

Strive to enter in at the strait gate: for many, I say unto you, will seek to enter in, and shall not be able. When once the master of the house is risen up, and hath shut to the door, and ye begin to stand without, and to knock at the door, saying, Lord, Lord, open unto us; and he shall answer and say unto you, I know you not whence ye are. *Luke 13:24–25*

Yet a little while is the light with you. Walk while ye have the light, lest darkness come upon you: for he that walketh in darkness knoweth not whither he goeth. *John 12:35*

But seek ye first the kingdom of God, and his righteousness; and all these things shall be added unto you. *Matthew 6:33*

Behold, now is the accepted time; behold, now is the day of salvation.   *2 Corinthians 6:2*

To day if ye will hear his voice, harden not your hearts.   *Hebrews 3:15*

Remember now thy Creator in the days of thy youth, while the evil days come not, nor the years draw nigh, when thou shalt say, I have no pleasure in them.   *Ecclesiastes 12:1*

He that is not with me is against me; and he that gathereth not with me scattereth abroad.   *Matthew 12:30*

5. I don't want you to talk to me about Christ.

He that despised Moses' law died without mercy under two or three witnesses: of how much sorer punishment, suppose ye, shall he be thought worthy, who hath trodden under foot the Son of God, and hath counted the blood of the covenant, wherewith he was sanctified, an unholy thing, and hath done despite unto the Spirit of grace?   *Hebrews 10:28–29*

See that ye refuse not him that speaketh. For if they escaped not who refused him that spake on earth, much more shall not we escape, if we turn away from him that speaketh from heaven. *Hebrews 12:25*

He that believeth and is baptized shall be saved; but he that believeth not shall be damned. *Mark 16:16*

For that they hated knowledge, and did not choose the fear of the LORD: they would none of my counsel: they despised all my reproof. Therefore shall they eat of the fruit of their own way, and be filled with their own devices. For the turning away of the simple shall slay them, and the prosperity of fools shall destroy them. But whoso hearkeneth unto me shall dwell safely, and shall be quiet from fear of evil. *Proverbs 1:29–33*

6. There is someone I can't forgive.

But if ye forgive not men their trespasses, neither will your Father forgive your trespasses. *Matthew 6:15*

Therefore is the kingdom of heaven likened unto a certain king, which would take account of his servants. And when he had begun to reckon, one was brought unto him, which owed him ten thousand talents. But forasmuch as he had not to pay, his lord commanded him to be sold, and his wife, and children, and all that he had, and payment to be made. The servant therefore fell down, and worshipped him, saying, Lord, have patience with me, and I will pay thee all. Then the lord of that servant was moved with compassion, and loosed him, and forgave him the debt. But the same servant went out, and found one of his fellowservants, which owed him an hundred pence: and he laid hands on him, and took him by the throat, saying, Pay me that thou owest. And his fellowservant fell down at his feet, and besought him, saying, Have patience with me, and I will pay thee all. And he would not: but went and cast him into prison, till he should pay the debt. So when his fellowservants saw what was done, they were very sorry, and came and told unto their lord all that was done. Then his lord, after that he had called him, said unto him, O thou wicked servant, I forgave thee all that debt, because thou desiredst me: shouldest not thou also have had compassion on thy fellowservant, even as I had pity on thee? And his lord was wroth, and delivered him to the tormentors, till he should pay all that was due unto him. So likewise shall my heavenly Father do also unto you, if ye from your hearts

forgive not every one his brother their trespasses.   *Matthew 18:23–35*

And be ye kind one to another, tender-
hearted, forgiving one another, even as God for
Christ's sake hath forgiven you.

Ephesians 4:32

I can do all things through Christ which
strengtheneth me.   *Philippians 4:13*

Special Texts for Special People

1. I'm a Roman Catholic.

Jesus answered and said unto him, Verily, verily, I say unto thee, Except a man be born again, he cannot see the kingdom of God....Verily, verily, I say unto thee, Except a man be born of water and of the Spirit, he cannot enter into the kingdom of God.... Marvel not that I said unto thee, Ye must be born again.   *John 3:3, 5, 7*

Whosoever is born of God doth not commit sin; for his seed remaineth in him: and he cannot sin, because he is born of God....We know that we have passed from death unto life, because we love the brethren. He that loveth not his brother abideth in death. Whosoever hateth his brother is a murderer: and ye know that no murderer hath eternal life abiding in him.

Hereby perceive we the love of God, because he laid down his life for us: and we ought to lay down our lives for the brethren. But whoso hath this world's good, and seeth his brother have need, and shutteth up his bowels of compassion from him, how dwelleth the love of God in him?

1 John 3:9, 14–17

But to him that worketh not, but believeth on him that justifieth the ungodly, his faith is counted for righteousness.   *Romans 4:5*

For there is one God, and one mediator between God and men, the man Christ Jesus.

1 Timothy 2:5

I acknowledged my sin unto thee, and mine iniquity have I not hid. I said, I will confess my transgressions unto the LORD; and thou forgavest the iniquity of my sin.

Psalm 32:5

These things have I written unto you that believe on the name of the Son of God; that ye may know that ye have eternal life.

1 John 5:13

And by him all that believe are justified from all things, from which ye could not be justified by the law of Moses.   *Acts 13:39*

Search the scriptures; for in them ye think ye have eternal life: and they are they which testify of me.   *John 5:39*

Wherefore laying aside all malice, and all guile, and hypocrisies, and envies, and all evil speakings, as newborn babes, desire the sincere milk of the word, that ye may grow thereby.   *1 Peter 2:1–2*

But evil men and seducers shall wax worse and worse, deceiving, and being deceived. But continue thou in the things which thou hast learned and hast been assured of, knowing of whom thou hast learned them; and that from a child thou hast known the holy scriptures, which are able to make thee wise unto salvation through faith which is in Christ Jesus. All scripture is given by inspiration of God, and is profitable for doctrine, for reproof, for correction, for instruction in righteousness: that the man of God may be perfect, thoroughly furnished unto all good works.

2 Timothy 3:13–17

Howbeit in vain do they worship me, teaching for doctrines the commandments of men. For laying aside the commandment of God, ye hold the tradition of men, as the washing of pots and cups: and many other such like things ye do...making the word of God of none effect through your tradition, which ye have delivered: and many such like things do ye.   *Mark 7:7-8, 13*

Ye do err, not knowing the scriptures, nor the power of God.   *Matthew 22:29*

2. I'm a Jew.

Who hath believed our report? and to whom is the arm of the LORD revealed? For he shall grow up before him as a tender plant, and as a root out of a dry ground: he hath no form nor comeliness; and when we shall see him, there is no beauty that we should desire him. He is despised and rejected of men; a man of sorrows, and acquainted with grief: and we hid as it were our faces from him; he was despised, and we esteemed him not. Surely he hath borne our griefs, and carried our sorrows: yet we did esteem him stricken, smitten of God, and afflicted. But he was wounded for our transgressions, he was bruised for our iniquities: the chastisement of our peace was upon him; and with his stripes we are healed. All we like sheep have gone astray; we have turned every one to his own way; and the LORD hath laid on him the iniquity of us all. He was oppressed, and he was afflicted, yet he opened not his mouth: he is brought as a lamb to the slaughter, and as a sheep before her shearers is dumb, so he openeth not his mouth. He was taken from prison and from judgment: and who shall declare his generation? for he was cut off out of the land of the living: for the transgression of my people was he stricken. And he made his grave with the wicked, and with the rich in his death; because he had done no violence, neither was any deceit in his mouth. Yet it pleased the LORD to bruise him; he hath put him to grief: when thou shalt make his soul an offering for sin, he shall see his seed, he shall prolong his days, and the pleasure of the LORD shall prosper in his hand. He shall see of the travail of his soul, and shall be satisfied: by his knowledge shall my righteous servant justify many; for he shall bear their iniquities. Therefore will I divide him a portion with the great, and he shall divide the spoil with the strong; because he hath poured out his soul unto death: and he was numbered with the transgressors; and he bare the sin of many, and made intercession for the trans- gressors.   *Isaiah 53*

And I will pour upon the house of David, and upon the inhabitants of Jerusalem, the spirit of grace and of supplications: and they shall look upon me whom they have pierced, and they shall mourn for him, as one mourneth for his only son, and shall be in bitterness for him, as one that is in bitterness for his firstborn.   *Zechariah 12:10*

And after threescore and two weeks shall Messiah be cut off, but not for himself: and the people of the prince that shall come shall destroy the city and the sanctuary; and the end thereof shall be with a flood, and unto the end of the war desolations are determined.

Daniel 9:26

3. I'm a spiritualist.

And when they shall say unto you, Seek unto them that have familiar spirits, and unto wizards that peep, and that mutter: should not a people seek unto their God? for the living to the dead? To the law and to the testimony: if they speak not according to this word, it is because there is no light in them. *Isaiah 8:19–20*

Beloved, believe not every spirit, but try the spirits whether they are of God: because many false prophets are gone out into the world. Hereby know ye the Spirit of God: Every spirit that confesseth that Jesus Christ is come in the flesh is of God: and every spirit that confesseth not that Jesus Christ is come in the flesh is not of God: and this is that spirit of antichrist, whereof ye have heard that it should come; and even now already is it in the world.   *1 John 4:1-3*

Regard not them that have familiar spirits, neither seek after wizards, to be defiled by them: I am the LORD your God.
                                        Leviticus 19:31

And the soul that turneth after such as have familiar spirits, and after wizards, to go a whoring after them, I will even set my face against that soul, and will cut him off from among his people.   *Leviticus 20:6*

There shall not be found among you any one that maketh his son or his daughter to pass through the fire, or that useth divination, or an observer of times, or an enchanter, or a witch, or a charmer, or a consulter with familiar spirits, or a wizard, or a necromancer. For all that do these things are an abomination unto the LORD: and because of these abominations the LORD thy God doth drive them out from before thee.   *Deuteronomy 18:10-12*

Then shall that Wicked be revealed...even him, whose coming is after the working of Satan with all power and signs and lying wonders, and with all deceivableness of unrighteousness in them that perish; because they received not the love of the truth, that they might be saved. And for this cause God shall send them strong delusion, that they should believe a lie: that they all might be damned who believed not the truth, but had pleasure in unrighteousness.

2 Thessalonians 2:8–12

So Saul died for his transgression which he committed against the LORD, even against the word of the LORD, which he kept not, and also for asking counsel of one that had a familiar spirit, to inquire of it; and inquired not of the LORD: therefore he slew him, and turned the kingdom unto David the son of Jesse.

1 Chronicles 10:13–14

Becoming a
Mature Believer

1. Confessing Christ before the World

Whosoever therefore shall confess me before men, him will I confess also before my Father which is in heaven. But whosoever shall deny me before men, him will I also deny before my Father which is in heaven.

Matthew 10:32–33

If thou shalt confess with thy mouth the Lord Jesus, and shalt believe in thine heart that God hath raised him from the dead, thou shalt be saved. For with the heart man believeth unto righteousness; and with the mouth confession is made unto salvation.

Romans 10:9–10

Nevertheless among the chief rulers also many believed on him; but because of the

84

Pharisees they did not confess him, lest they should be put out of the synagogue: for they loved the praise of men more than the praise of God.   *John 12:42–43*

Whosoever therefore shall be ashamed of me and of my words in this adulterous and sinful generation; of him also shall the Son of man be ashamed, when he cometh in the glory of his Father with the holy angels.   *Mark 8:38*

2. The Bible—God's Message to Man

As newborn babes, desire the sincere milk of the word, that ye may grow thereby.
                                        1 Peter 2:2

And now, brethren, I commend you to God, and to the word of his grace, which is able to build you up, and to give you an inheritance among all them which are sanctified.
                                        Acts 20:32

Wherefore lay apart all filthiness and superfluity of naughtiness, and receive with meekness the engrafted word, which is able to save your souls. But be ye doers of the word, and not hearers only, deceiving your own selves.   *James 1:21–22*

All scripture is given by inspiration of God, and is profitable for doctrine, for reproof, for correction, for instruction in righteousness: that the man of God may be perfect, thoroughly furnished unto all good works.

2 Timothy 3:16–17

And take the helmet of salvation, and the sword of the Spirit, which is the word of God.

Ephesians 6:17

Wherewithal shall a young man cleanse his way? by taking heed thereto according to thy word....Thy word have I hid in mine heart, that I might not sin against thee....The entrance of thy words giveth light; it giveth understanding unto the simple.

Psalm 119:9, 11, 130

Blessed is the man that walketh not in the counsel of the ungodly, nor standeth in the way of sinners, nor sitteth in the seat of the scornful. But his delight is in the law of the LORD; and in his law doth he meditate day and night.

Psalm 1:1–2

This book of the law shall not depart out of thy mouth; but thou shalt meditate therein day and night, that thou mayest observe to do according to all that is written therein: for then thou shalt make thy way prosperous, and then thou shalt have good success.   *Joshua 1:8*

These were more noble than those in Thessalonica, in that they received the word with all readiness of mind, and searched the scriptures daily, whether those things were so.
Acts 17:11

3. The Privilege of Prayer

Ye lust, and have not: ye kill, and desire to have, and cannot obtain: ye fight and war, yet ye have not, because ye ask not.   *James 4:2*

Ask, and it shall be given you; seek, and ye shall find; knock, and it shall be opened unto you. For every one that asketh receiveth; and he that seeketh findeth; and to him that knocketh it shall be opened. If a son shall ask bread of any of you that is a father, will he give him a stone? or if he ask a fish, will he for a fish give him a serpent? Or if he shall ask an egg, will he offer him a scorpion? If ye then, being evil, know how to give good gifts unto your children: how much more shall your heavenly Father give the Holy Spirit to them that ask him?   *Luke 11:9–13*

Is any among you afflicted? let him pray. Is any merry? let him sing psalms. Is any sick among you? let him call for the elders of the church; and let them pray over him, anointing him with oil in the name of the Lord: and the prayer of faith shall save the sick, and the Lord shall raise him up; and if he have committed sins, they shall be forgiven him. Confess your faults one to another, and pray one for another, that ye may be healed. The effectual fervent prayer of a righteous man availeth much. Elias was a man subject to like passions as we are, and he prayed earnestly that it might not rain: and it rained not on the earth by the space of three years and six months. And he prayed again, and the heaven gave rain, and the earth brought forth her fruit.

James 5:13–18

Why sleep ye? rise and pray, lest ye enter into temptation. *Luke 22:46*

But they that wait upon the LORD shall renew their strength; they shall mount up with wings as eagles; they shall run, and not be weary; and they shall walk, and not faint.

Isaiah 40:31

Evening, and morning, and at noon, will I pray, and cry aloud: and he shall hear my voice. *Psalm 55:17*

Now when Daniel knew that the writing was signed, he went into his house; and his windows being open in his chamber toward Jerusalem, he kneeled upon his knees three times a day, and prayed, and gave thanks before his God, as he did aforetime.   *Daniel 6:10*

And when [Jesus] had sent them away, he departed into a mountain to pray.   *Mark 6:46*

And it came to pass in those days, that [Jesus] went out into a mountain to pray, and continued all night in prayer to God.
Luke 6:12

Pray without ceasing.
1 Thessalonians 5:17

4. Living a Holy Life

Be ye not unequally yoked together with unbelievers: for what fellowship hath righteousness with unrighteousness? and what communion hath light with darkness? And what concord hath Christ with Belial? or what part hath he that believeth with an infidel? And what agreement hath the temple of God with idols? for ye are the temple of the living God; as God hath said, I will dwell in them, and walk in them; and I will be their God, and they shall be my people. Wherefore come out from among them, and be ye separate, saith the Lord, and touch not the unclean thing; and I will receive you, and will be a Father unto you, and ye shall be my sons and daughters, saith the Lord Almighty. Having therefore these promises, dearly beloved, let us cleanse ourselves from all filthiness of the flesh and spirit, perfecting holiness in the fear of God.

2 Corinthians 6:14–7:1

No man can serve two masters: for either he will hate the one, and love the other; or else he will hold to the one, and despise the other. Ye cannot serve God and mammon.

Matthew 6:24

Love not the world, neither the things that are in the world. If any man love the world, the love of the Father is not in him. For all that is in the world, the lust of the flesh, and the lust of the eyes, and the pride of life, is not of the Father, but is of the world. And the world passeth away, and the lust thereof: but he that doeth the will of God abideth for ever.

1 John 2:15–17

Know ye not that the friendship of the world is enmity with God? whosoever therefore will be a friend of the world is the enemy of

God....But he giveth more grace. Wherefore he saith, God resisteth the proud, but giveth grace unto the humble. Submit yourselves therefore to God. Resist the devil, and he will flee from you. Draw nigh to God, and he will draw nigh to you. Cleanse your hands, ye sinners; and purify your hearts, ye double minded.

James 4:4, 6–8

Follow peace with all men, and holiness, without which no man shall see the Lord.

Hebrews 12:14

As obedient children, not fashioning yourselves according to the former lusts in your ignorance: but as he which hath called you is holy, so be ye holy in all manner of conversation; because it is written, Be ye holy; for I am holy. And if ye call on the Father, who without respect of persons judgeth according to every man's work, pass the time of your sojourning here in fear: forasmuch as ye know that ye were not redeemed with corruptible things, as silver and gold, from your vain conversation received by tradition from your fathers; but with the precious blood of Christ, as of a lamb without blemish and without spot. *1 Peter 1:14–19*

For the time is come that judgment must begin at the house of God: and if it first begin at us, what shall the end be of them that obey not the gospel of God? And if the righteous scarcely be saved, where shall the ungodly and the sinner appear?   *1 Peter 4:17–18*

And that which fell among thorns are they, which, when they have heard, go forth, and are choked with cares and riches and pleasures of this life, and bring no fruit to perfection.   *Luke 8:14*

Take heed to yourselves, lest at any time your hearts be overcharged with surfeiting, and drunkenness, and cares of this life, and so that day come upon you unawares. For as a snare shall it come on all them that dwell on the face of the whole earth. Watch ye therefore, and pray always, that ye may be accounted worthy to escape all these things that shall come to pass, and to stand before the Son of man.   *Luke 21:34–36*

I beseech you therefore, brethren, by the mercies of God, that ye present your bodies a living sacrifice, holy, acceptable unto God, which is your reasonable service. And be not conformed to this world: but be ye transformed by the renewing of your mind, that ye may prove what is that good, and acceptable, and perfect, will of God.   *Romans 12:1–2*

I have fought a good fight, I have finished my course, I have kept the faith: henceforth there is laid up for me a crown of righteousness, which the Lord, the righteous judge, shall give me at that day: and not to me only, but unto all them also that love his appearing.

2 Timothy 4:7-8

5. Working for Christ

For the Son of man is as a man taking a far journey, who left his house, and gave authority to his servants, and to every man his work, and commanded the porter to watch. Watch ye therefore: for ye know not when the master of the house cometh, at even, or at midnight, or at the cockcrowing, or in the morning: lest coming suddenly he find you sleeping. And what I say unto you I say unto all, Watch.

Mark 13:34-37

Therefore be ye also ready: for in such an hour as ye think not the Son of man cometh. Who then is a faithful and wise servant, whom his lord hath made ruler over his household, to give them meat in due season? Blessed is that servant, whom his lord when he cometh shall find so doing. Verily I say unto you, That he shall make him ruler over all his goods. But and if that evil servant shall say in his heart, My lord delayeth his coming; and shall begin to smite his fellowservants, and to eat and drink with the drunken; the lord of that servant shall come in a day when he looketh not for him, and in an hour that he is not aware of, and shall cut him asunder, and appoint him his portion with the hypocrites: there shall be weeping and gnashing of teeth. *Matthew 24:44–51*

For the kingdom of heaven is as a man travelling into a far country, who called his own servants, and delivered unto them his goods. And unto one he gave five talents, to another two, and to another one; to every man according to his several ability; and straightway took his journey. Then he that had received the five talents went and traded with the same, and made them other five talents. And likewise he that had received two, he also gained other two. But he that had received one went and digged in the earth, and hid his lord's money. After a long time the lord of those servants cometh, and reckoneth with them. And so he that had received five talents came and brought other five talents, saying, Lord, thou deliveredst unto me five talents: behold, I have gained beside them five talents more. His lord said unto him, Well done, thou good and faithful servant: thou hast been faithful over a few things, I will make thee ruler over many things: enter thou into the joy of thy lord. He also that had received two talents came and said, Lord, thou deliveredst unto me two talents: behold, I have gained two other talents beside them. His lord said unto him, Well done, good and faithful servant; thou hast been faithful over a few things, I will make thee ruler over many things: enter thou into the joy of thy lord. Then he which had received the one talent came and said, Lord, I knew thee that thou art an hard man, reaping where thou hast not sown, and gathering where thou hast not strowed: and I was afraid, and went and hid thy talent in the earth: lo, there thou hast that is thine. His lord answered and said unto him, Thou wicked and slothful servant, thou knewest that I reap where I sowed not, and gather where I have not strowed: thou oughtest therefore to have put my money to the exchangers, and then at my coming I should have received mine own with usury. Take therefore the talent from him, and give it unto him which hath ten talents. For unto every one that hath shall be given, and he shall have abundance: but from him that hath not shall be taken away even that which he hath. And cast ye the unprofitable servant into outer darkness: there shall be weeping and gnashing of teeth. *Matthew 25:14–30*

Therefore they that were scattered abroad went every where preaching the word.   *Acts 8:4*

That we henceforth be no more children, tossed to and fro, and carried about with every wind of doctrine, by the sleight of men, and cunning craftiness, whereby they lie in wait to deceive; but speaking the truth in love, may grow up into him in all things, which is the head, even Christ: from whom the whole body fitly joined together and compacted by that which every joint supplieth, according to the effectual working in the measure of every part, maketh increase of the body unto the edifying of itself in love.   *Ephesians 4:14–16*

Awake thou that sleepest, and arise from the dead, and Christ shall give thee light. See then that ye walk circumspectly, not as fools, but as wise, redeeming the time, because the days are evil. Wherefore be ye not unwise, but understanding what the will of the Lord is. And be not drunk with wine, wherein is excess; but be filled with the Spirit; speaking to yourselves in psalms and hymns and spiritual songs, singing and making melody in your heart to the Lord; giving thanks always for all things unto God and the Father in the name of our Lord Jesus Christ; submitting yourselves one to another in the fear of God.   *Ephesians 5:14–21*

Let him know, that he which converteth the sinner from the error of his way shall save a soul from death, and shall hide a multitude of sins. *James 5:20*

And they that be wise shall shine as the brightness of the firmament; and they that turn many to righteousness as the stars for ever and ever. *Daniel 12:3*

And, behold, I come quickly; and my reward is with me, to give every man according as his work shall be. *Revelation 22:12*

Strength for Difficult Times

1. Victory over Temptation

My brethren, count it all joy when ye fall into divers temptations; knowing this, that the trying of your faith worketh patience. But let patience have her perfect work, that ye may be perfect and entire, wanting nothing.

James 1:2–4

Blessed is the man that endureth temptation: for when he is tried, he shall receive the crown of life, which the Lord hath promised to them that love him.   *James 1:12*

Be sober, be vigilant; because your adversary the devil, as a roaring lion, walketh about, seeking whom he may devour: whom resist stedfast in the faith, knowing that the same afflictions are accomplished in your brethren that are in the world. But the God of all grace, who hath called us unto his eternal glory by Christ Jesus, after that ye have suffered a while, make you perfect, stablish, strengthen, settle you.   *1 Peter 5:8–10*

There hath no temptation taken you but such as is common to man: but God is faithful, who will not suffer you to be tempted above that ye are able; but will with the temptation also make a way to escape, that ye may be able to bear it.   *1 Corinthians 10:13*

And he said unto me, My grace is sufficient for thee: for my strength is made perfect in weakness. Most gladly therefore will I rather glory in my infirmities, that the power of Christ may rest upon me. Therefore I take pleasure in infirmities, in reproaches, in necessities, in persecutions, in distresses for Christ's sake: for when I am weak, then am I strong.
                          2 Corinthians 12:9–10

Pray without ceasing.
                          1 Thessalonians 5:17

Every spirit that confesseth not that Jesus Christ is come in the flesh is not of God....Ye are of God, little children, and have overcome them: because greater is he that is in you, than he that is in the world.   *1 John 4:3–4*

I can do all things through Christ which strengtheneth me. *Philippians 4:13*

I have written unto you, fathers, because ye have known him that is from the beginning. I have written unto you, young men, because ye are strong, and the word of God abideth in you, and ye have overcome the wicked one.
1 John 2:14

Wherewithal shall a young man cleanse his way? by taking heed thereto according to thy word. *Psalm 119:9*

2. Rejoicing in Persecution

Blessed are they which are persecuted for righteousness' sake: for theirs is the kingdom of heaven. Blessed are ye, when men shall revile you, and persecute you, and shall say all manner of evil against you falsely, for my sake. Rejoice, and be exceeding glad: for great is your reward in heaven: for so persecuted they the prophets which were before you.
Matthew 5:10–12

Beloved, think it not strange concerning the fiery trial which is to try you, as though some strange thing happened unto you: but rejoice, inasmuch as ye are partakers of Christ's sufferings; that, when his glory shall be revealed, ye may be glad also with exceeding joy. If ye be reproached for the name of Christ, happy are ye; for the spirit of glory and of God resteth upon you: on their part he is evil spoken of, but on your part he is glorified.

1 Peter 4:12–14

If any man suffer as a Christian, let him not be ashamed; but let him glorify God on this behalf. *1 Peter 4:16*

For even hereunto were ye called: because Christ also suffered for us, leaving us an example, that ye should follow his steps...who, when he was reviled, reviled not again; when he suffered, he threatened not; but committed himself to him that judgeth righteously.

1 Peter 2:21, 23

For it is better, if the will of God be so, that ye suffer for well doing, than for evil doing. For Christ also hath once suffered for sins, the just for the unjust, that he might bring us to God, being put to death in the flesh, but quickened by the Spirit. *1 Peter 3:17–18*

Yea, and all that will live godly in Christ Jesus shall suffer persecution. *2 Timothy 3:12*

If we suffer, we shall also reign with him: if we deny him, he also will deny us.

2 Timothy 2:12

Continue in the faith...[for] we must through much tribulation enter into the kingdom of God.

Acts 14:22

And when they had called the apostles, and beaten them, they commanded that they should not speak in the name of Jesus, and let them go. And they departed from the presence of the council, rejoicing that they were counted worthy to suffer shame for his name. And daily in the temple, and in every house, they ceased not to teach and preach Jesus Christ.

Acts 5:40–42

Wherefore seeing we also are compassed about with so great a cloud of witnesses, let us lay aside every weight, and the sin which doth so easily beset us, and let us run with patience the race that is set before us, looking unto Jesus the author and finisher of our faith; who for the joy that was set before him endured the cross, despising the shame, and is set down at the right hand of the throne of God. For consider him that endured such contradiction of sinners against himself, lest ye be wearied and faint in your minds. Ye have not yet resisted unto blood, striving against sin. *Hebrews 12:1-4*

Fear none of those things which thou shalt suffer: behold, the devil shall cast some of you into prison, that ye may be tried; and ye shall have tribulation ten days: be thou faithful unto death, and I will give thee a crown of life.

Revelation 2:10

3. Persevering through Trial

An inheritance incorruptible, and undefiled, and that fadeth not away [is] reserved in heaven for you, who are kept by the power of God through faith unto salvation ready to be revealed in the last time. Wherein ye greatly rejoice, though now for a season, if need be, ye are in heaviness through manifold temptations: that the trial of your faith, being much more precious than of gold that perisheth, though it be tried with fire, might be found unto praise and honour and glory at the appearing of Jesus Christ. *1 Peter 1:4-7*

Humble yourselves therefore under the mighty hand of God, that he may exalt you in due time: casting all your care upon him; for he careth for you. *1 Peter 5:6-7*

God is our refuge and strength, a very present help in trouble. Therefore will not we fear, though the earth be removed, and though the mountains be carried into the midst of the sea; though the waters thereof roar and be troubled, though the mountains shake with the swelling thereof.   *Psalm 46:1–3*

Yea, though I walk through the valley of the shadow of death, I will fear no evil: for thou art with me; thy rod and thy staff they comfort me.   *Psalm 23:4*

Many are the afflictions of the righteous: but the LORD delivereth him out of them all.
                                          Psalm 34:19

Call upon me in the day of trouble: I will deliver thee, and thou shalt glorify me.
                                          Psalm 50:15

The righteous cry, and the LORD heareth, and delivereth them out of all their troubles.
                                          Psalm 34:17

The LORD is my light and my salvation; whom shall I fear? the LORD is the strength of my life; of whom shall I be afraid? When the wicked, even mine enemies and my foes, came upon me to eat up my flesh, they stumbled and fell. Though an host should encamp against me, my heart shall not fear: though war should rise against me, in this will I be confident. One thing have I desired of the LORD, that will I seek after; that I may dwell in the house of the LORD all the days of my life, to behold the beauty of the LORD, and to inquire in his temple. For in the time of trouble he shall hide me in his pavilion: in the secret of his tabernacle shall he hide me; he shall set me up upon a rock. And now shall mine head be lifted up above mine enemies round about me: therefore will I offer in his tabernacle sacrifices of joy; I will sing, yea, I will sing praises unto the LORD....I had fainted, unless I had believed to see the goodness of the LORD in the land of the living. Wait on the LORD: be of good courage, and he shall strengthen thine heart: wait, I say, on the LORD.   *Psalm 27:1–6, 13–14*

Come unto me, all ye that labour and are heavy laden, and I will give you rest. Take my yoke upon you, and learn of me; for I am meek and lowly in heart: and ye shall find rest unto your souls.   *Matthew 11:28–29*

4. Comfort in Time of Loss

Let not your heart be troubled: ye believe in God, believe also in me. In my Father's house are many mansions: if it were not so, I would have told you. I go to prepare a place for you. And if I go and prepare a place for you, I will come again, and receive you unto myself; that where I am, there ye may be also....Peace I leave with you, my peace I give unto you: not as the world giveth, give I unto you. Let not your heart be troubled, neither let it be afraid.

John 14:1–3, 27

Be still, and know that I am God.

Psalm 46:10

And I heard a voice from heaven saying unto me, Write, Blessed are the dead which die in the Lord from henceforth: Yea, saith the Spirit, that they may rest from their labours; and their works do follow them.

Revelation 14:13

But I would not have you to be ignorant, brethren, concerning them which are asleep, that ye sorrow not, even as others which have no hope. For if we believe that Jesus died and rose again, even so them also which sleep in Jesus will God bring with him. For this we say unto you by the word of the Lord, that we which are alive and remain unto the coming of the Lord shall not prevent them which are asleep. For the Lord himself shall descend from heaven with a shout, with the voice of the archangel, and with the trump of God: and the dead in Christ shall rise first: then we which are alive and remain shall be caught up together with them in the clouds, to meet the Lord in the air: and so shall we ever be with the Lord. Wherefore comfort one another with these words. *1 Thessalonians 4:13–18*

Therefore we are always confident, knowing that, whilst we are at home in the body, we are absent from the Lord: (for we walk by faith, not by sight:) we are confident, I say, and willing rather to be absent from the body, and to be present with the Lord.

2 Corinthians 5:6–8

For I am in a strait betwixt two, having a desire to depart, and to be with Christ; which is far better. *Philippians 1:23*

For this corruptible must put on incorruption, and this mortal must put on immortality. So when this corruptible shall have put on incorruption, and this mortal shall have put on immortality, then shall be brought to pass the saying that is written, Death is swallowed up in victory. O death, where is thy sting? O grave, where is thy victory? The sting of death is sin; and the strength of sin is the law. But thanks be to God, which giveth us the victory through our Lord Jesus Christ. Therefore, my beloved brethren, be ye stedfast, unmoveable, always abounding in the work of the Lord, forasmuch as ye know that your labour is not in vain in the Lord. *1 Corinthians 15:53–58*

Helpful
Soul-Winning Hints

1. Generally deal with people of your own sex and close to your own age.

2. Whenever it is possible, talk to the person alone.

3. Rely completely on the Spirit of God.

4. Do not merely quote or read passages from the Bible, but have the one with whom you are speaking read them for himself.

5. Emphasize a single passage of Scripture, repeating and discussing it until the inquirer cannot forget it. He will hear it ringing in his memory long after you have ceased talking.

6. Always hold the person to the main point of accepting Christ. Many opportunities for repentance have been lost by an inexperienced worker allowing himself to become

involved in an argument over some side issue.

7. Be courteous. Some overzealous workers cause the people they approach to become defensive and to put up barriers that are impossible to penetrate.

8. Be earnest. Genuine earnestness means more than any skill learned in a training class or even from a book such as this.

9. Never lose your temper.

10. Never interrupt anyone else who is leading someone to Christ.

11. Don't be in a hurry.

12. Ask the person to pray with you. Difficulties can disappear during prayer, and many stubborn people yield when they are brought into the presence of God.

13. Whenever you seem to fail, go home, pray about it, and find out why you failed. Then go back, if you can, and try again.

14. Be sure to give the new believer definite instructions concerning how to succeed in the Christian life.

15. Spend time with the new believer regularly to encourage him and to help him grow as a Christian.

About the Author

Reuben Archer Torrey is respected as one of the greatest evangelists of modern times. Several years after his graduation from Yale Divinity School, he was selected by D. L. Moody to become the first dean of the Moody Bible Institute of Chicago. Under his direction, Moody Institute became a pattern for Bible institutes around the world.

Dr. Torrey spent the years of 1903–1905 in worldwide revival campaigns, winning thousands of souls to Jesus Christ. He continued worldwide crusades for the next fifteen years while he served as the dean of the Bible Institute of Los Angeles and pastored the Church of the Open Door in that city.

Torrey longed for more Christian workers to take an active part in bringing the message of salvation through Christ to a lost and dying world. His straightforward style of evangelism has shown thousands of Christian workers how to become effective soulwinners.

The Bible contains golden nuggets of truth, and anyone willing to dig for that truth is certain to find it. With its numerous study helps, this unique and indispensable reference tool will help all those who wish to understand and master the Scriptures. Torrey's methods for studying the Bible immediately silence the excuse, "I can't find time."

How to Study the Bible
R. A. Torrey
ISBN: 978-0-88368-164-0 • Pocket • 96 pages

Because prayer is so vital to your faith, it is essential that you comprehend God's methods of hearing and answering prayer. R. A. Torrey shares spiritual guidelines to prayer learned from years of seeking God and receiving answers. All who put his lessons into practice will find their prayer lives permanently altered.

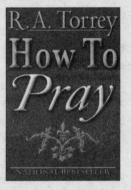

How to Pray
R. A. Torrey
ISBN: 978-0-88368-133-6 • Pocket • 112 pages